how LONG are they?

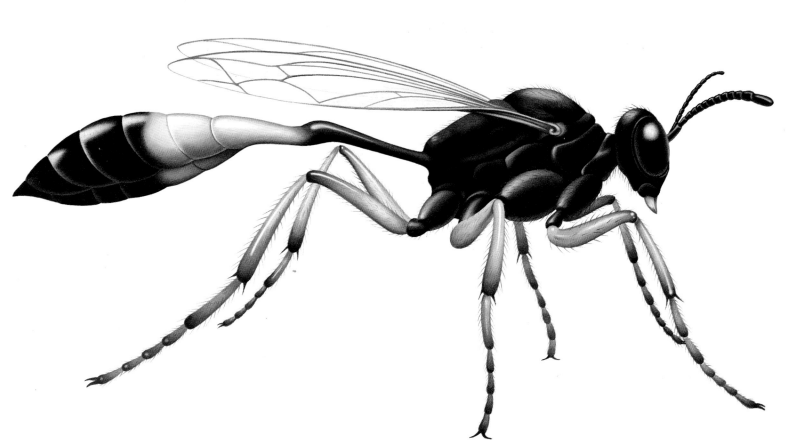

Orpheus

HOW TO USE THIS BOOK

For each double page, all the illustrations are drawn to scale. The longest thing is featured again on the following double page, where it appears as the *shortest* thing. (You can find it quickly because its label is contained in a box.) The illustrations on this double page are also all drawn to scale and the longest thing is again featured on the next double page. And so on, all the way through the book.

MEASUREMENTS

0.0001 millimetres *means* one ten-thousandth of a millimetre.
0.0015 millimetres *means* fifteen ten-thousandths of a millimetre.
0.25 millimetres *means* a quarter of a millimetre.
0.2 millimetres *means* one fifth of a millimetre
0.5 millimetres *means* a half of a millimetre.
10 millimetres *is the same as* 1 centimetre.
100 centimetres *is the same as* 1 metre
mm *is an abbreviation of* millimetre.
cm *is an abbreviation of* centimetre.
m *is an abbreviation of* metre.

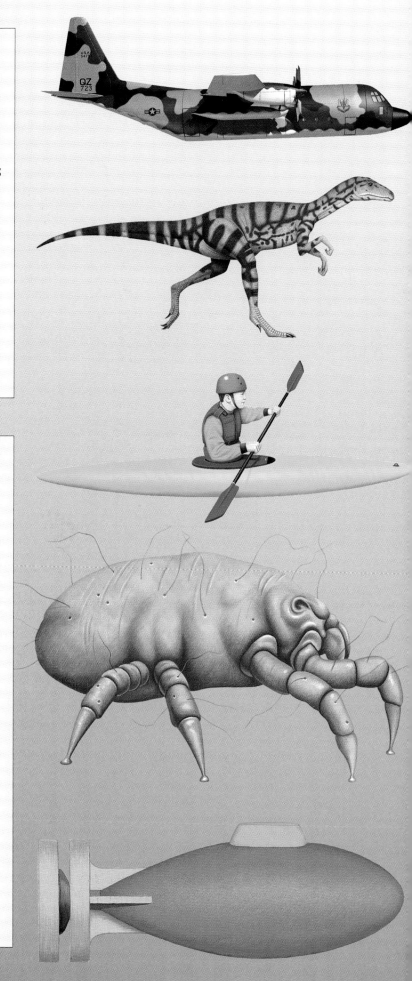

CONTENTS

6   **0.0001 – 0.0015 millimetres**
Virus • Bacterium

8   **0.0015 – 0.25 millimetres**
Bacterium • Tardigrade • Feather-winged beetle

10   **0.25 – 2 millimetres**
Feather-winged beetle • Dust mite • Ant larva • Parasitic wasp

12   **2 – 20 millimetres**
Parasitic wasp • Nematode worm • Medical submarine • Earwig • Dwarf gecko

14   **2 – 20 centimetres**
Dwarf gecko • Angler fish • Thread snake • Prairie vole • Child's foot

16   **20 centimetres – 1 metre**
Child's foot • Centipede • Duckbilled platypus • Nurse shark • *Eoraptor*

18   **1 – 2.7 metres**
Eoraptor • Japanese giant salamander • Leatherback turtle • Canoe • Conger eel

20   **2.7 – 7 metres**
Conger eel • Nile crocodile • Southern elephant seal • Great white shark

22   **7 – 33 metres**
Great white shark • *Diplodocus* • Transport aircraft • Blue whale

24   **33 – 70 metres**
Blue whale • Clipper ship • Road train • Boeing 777-200 • Passenger ferry

26   **70 – 256 metres**
Passenger ferry • Submarine • *Hindenburg* airship • *Titanic*

28   **256 – 1280 metres**
Titanic • Aircraft carrier • Oil tanker • Grand Coulee Dam • Golden Gate Bridge

30   **Index**

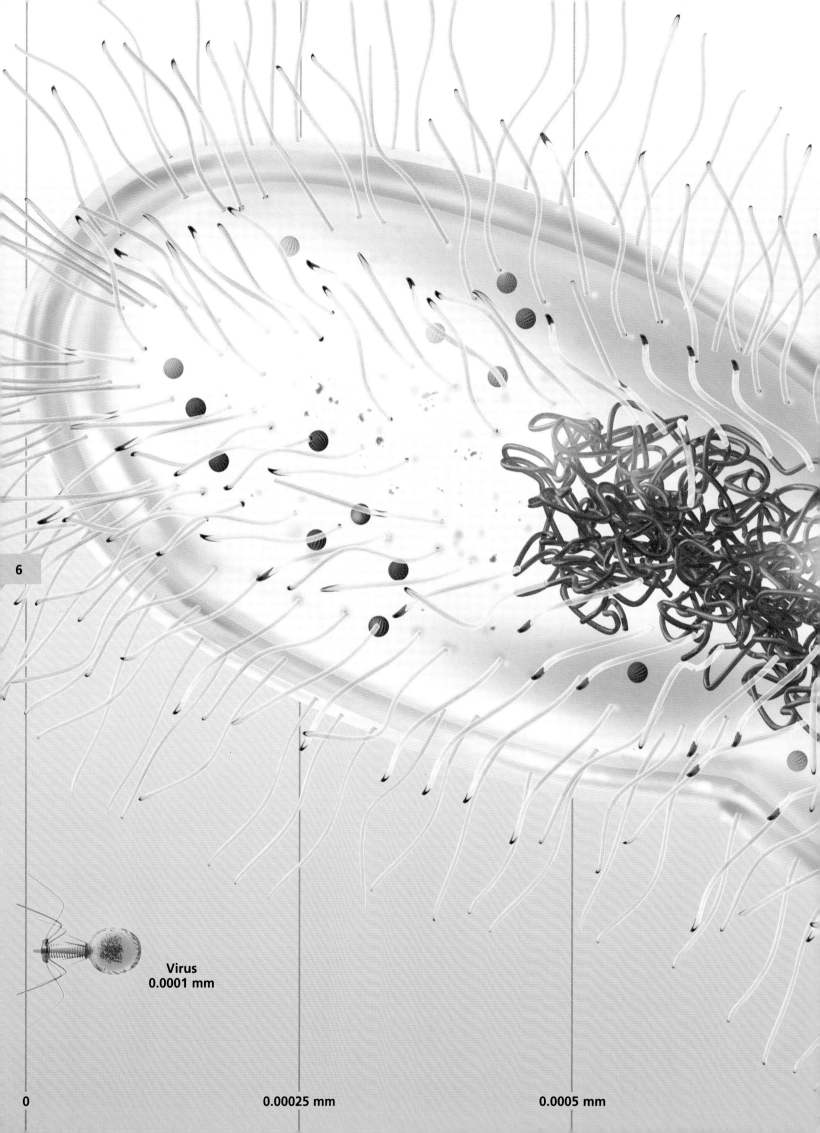

6

Virus
0.0001 mm

0

0.00025 mm

0.0005 mm

VIRUSES are the smallest living things. You can only observe them through special, powerful microscopes. They are little more than small bags of chemicals. They only start to live when they get inside cells, the microscopic "building blocks" of which all living things are made. Viruses use these cells to make copies of themselves. The common cold and measles are caused by viruses.

Some bacteria also cause disease, but most are harmless. Many kinds help recycle nutrients in the soil. Bacteria can be found floating in the air or at the bottom of the sea, in scalding water or frozen in ice. A quarter of million bacteria can fit on to a single pinhead!

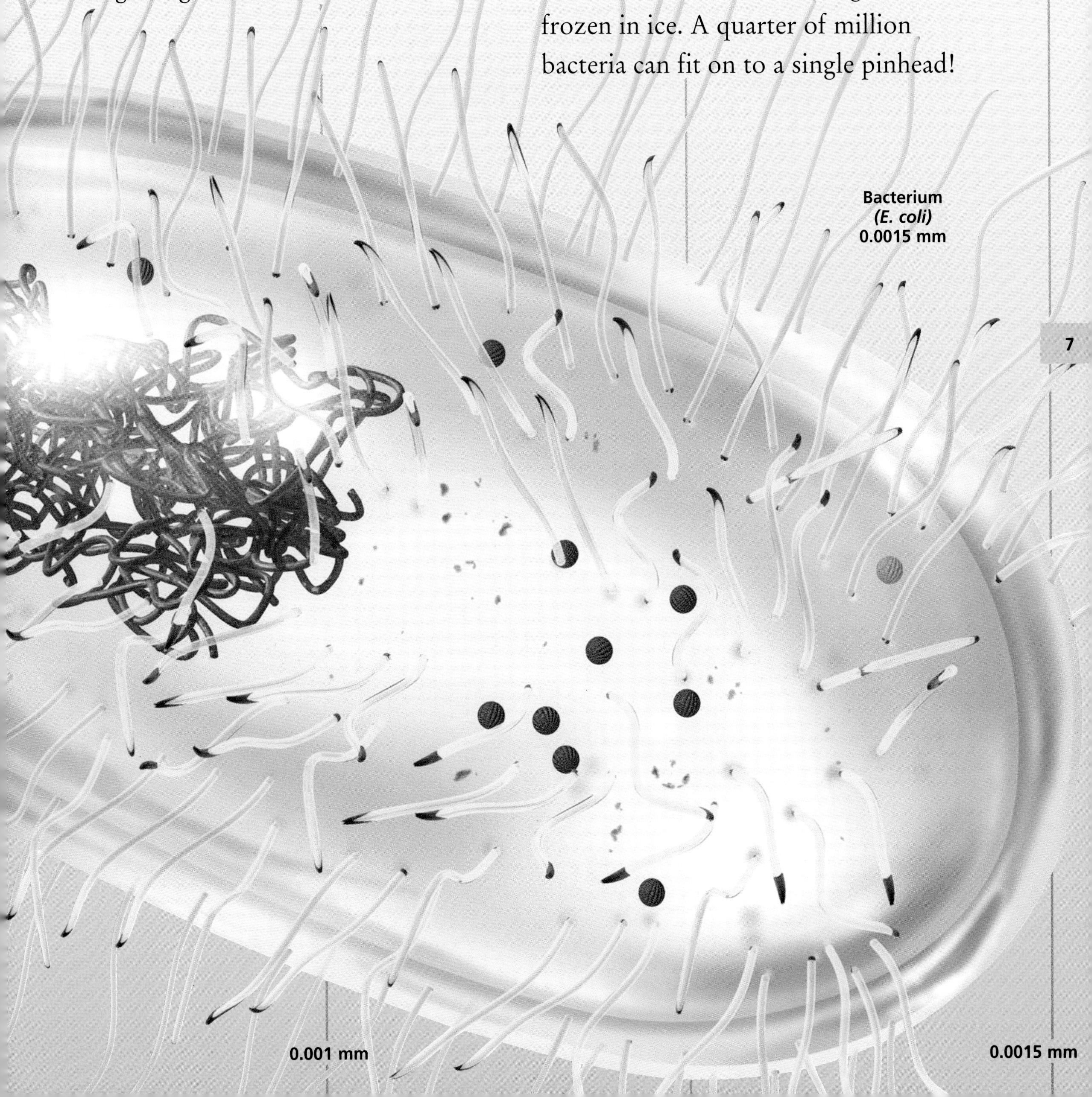

Bacterium
(*E. coli*)
0.0015 mm

7

0.001 mm

0.0015 mm

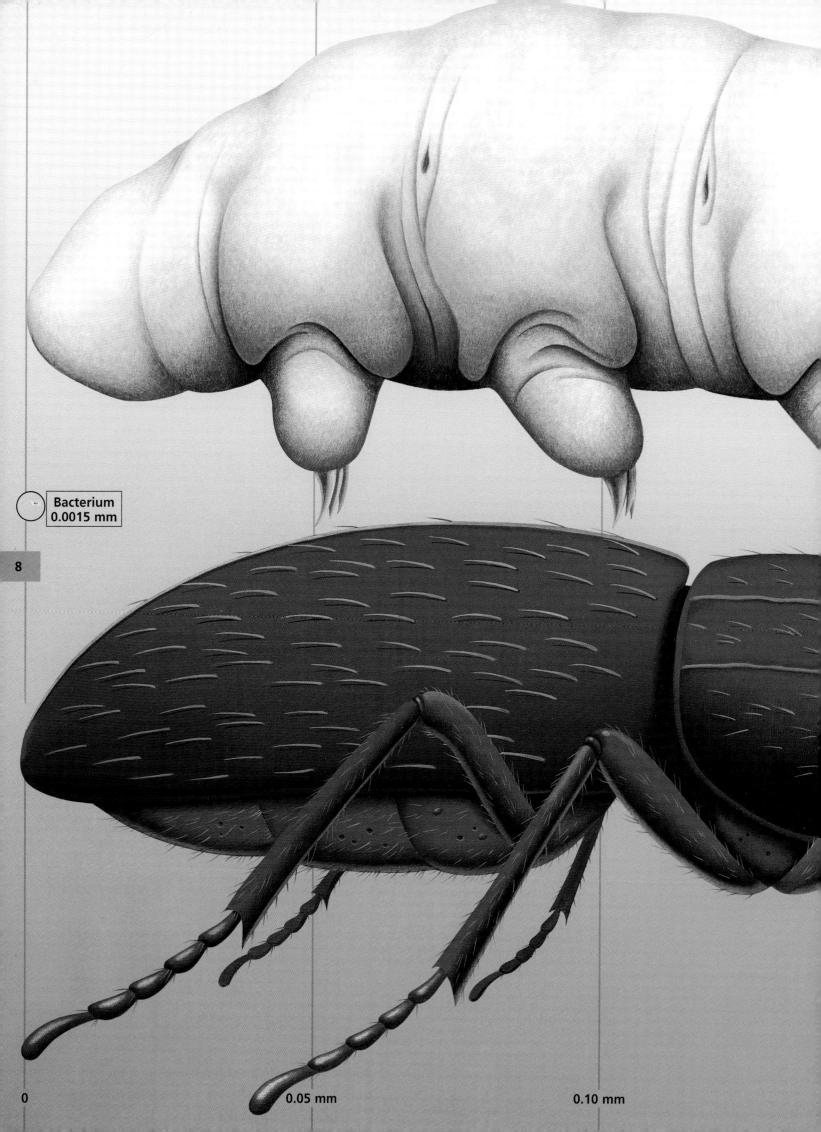

Bacterium
0.0015 mm

0   0.05 mm   0.10 mm

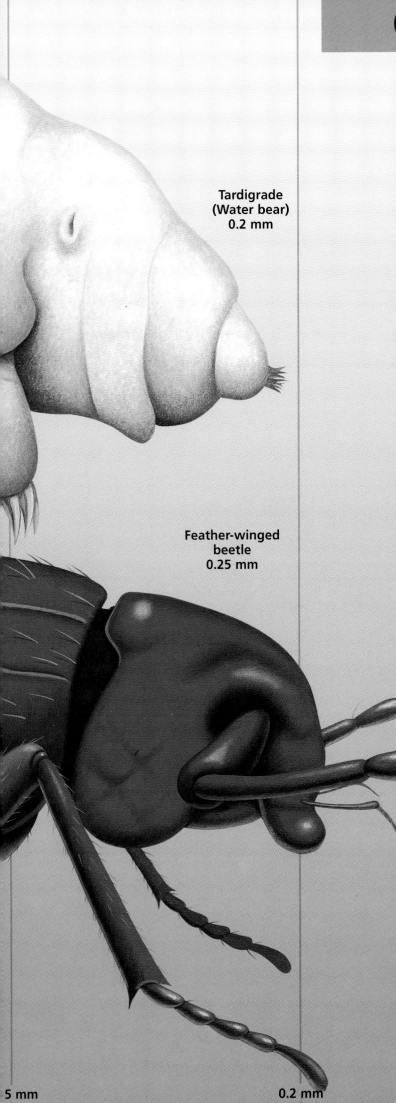

Tardigrade (Water bear) 0.2 mm

Feather-winged beetle 0.25 mm

THE TWO ANIMALS pictured on these pages are massive compared to a bacterium, yet they themselves can also only be properly observed through a microscope. Sometimes known as water bears, tardigrades live in places that are usually damp, such as in ponds or gutters, or in the thin film of water on plants. If these places should suddenly dry out, the tardigrade tucks its legs and head into a ball and goes into a state of deep sleep. It only comes to life again once the wetness returns. It can remain in its deep sleep for more than 25 years.

Feather-winged beetles are the smallest beetles in the world. All the features that they share with their larger relatives—including compound eyes, mouthparts, wings, antennae and so on—are packed into a creature a fraction of a millimetre long. They are named after their feather-tipped wings, which they use to help them float on water. Feather-winged beetles live under dead leaves or bark, in decaying logs, compost heaps, or treeholes, under seaweed on seashores, or in animal dung. They will live anywhere that the moulds and fungi upon which they feed also grow.

5 mm

0.2 mm

0.25 mm

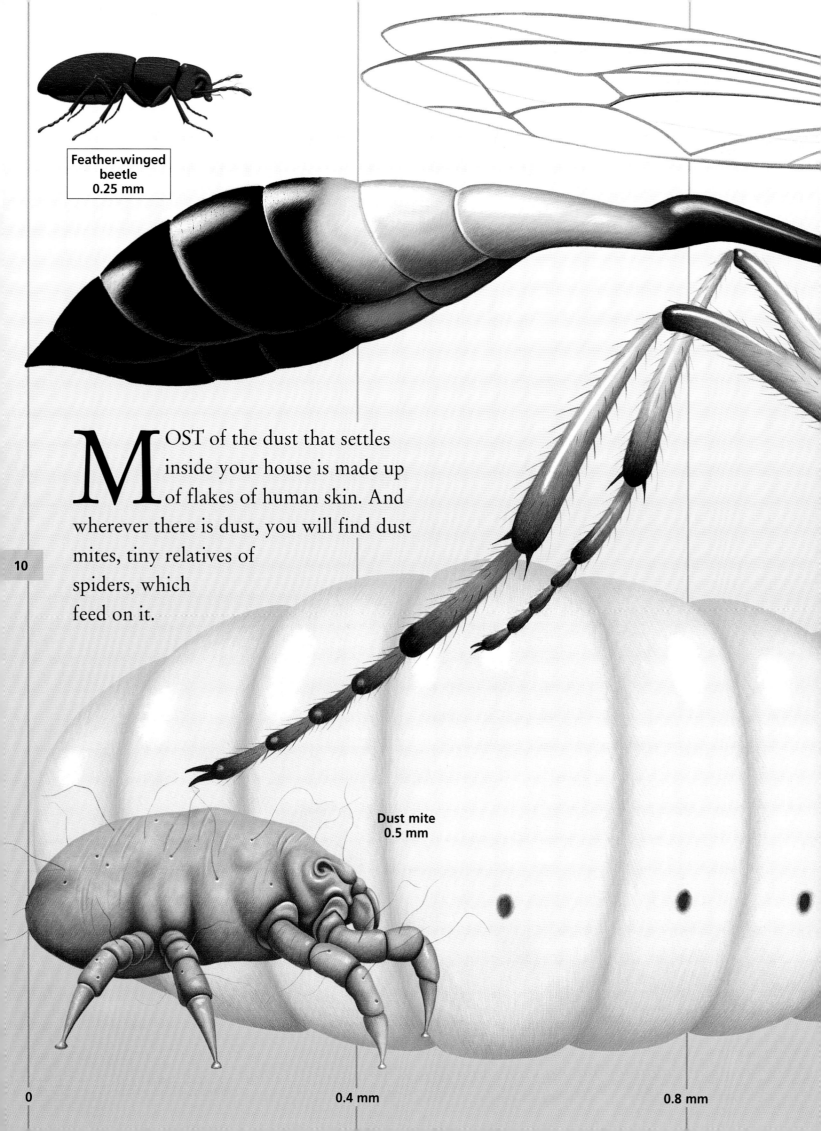

Feather-winged beetle 0.25 mm

MOST of the dust that settles inside your house is made up of flakes of human skin. And wherever there is dust, you will find dust mites, tiny relatives of spiders, which feed on it.

Dust mite 0.5 mm

0

0.4 mm

0.8 mm

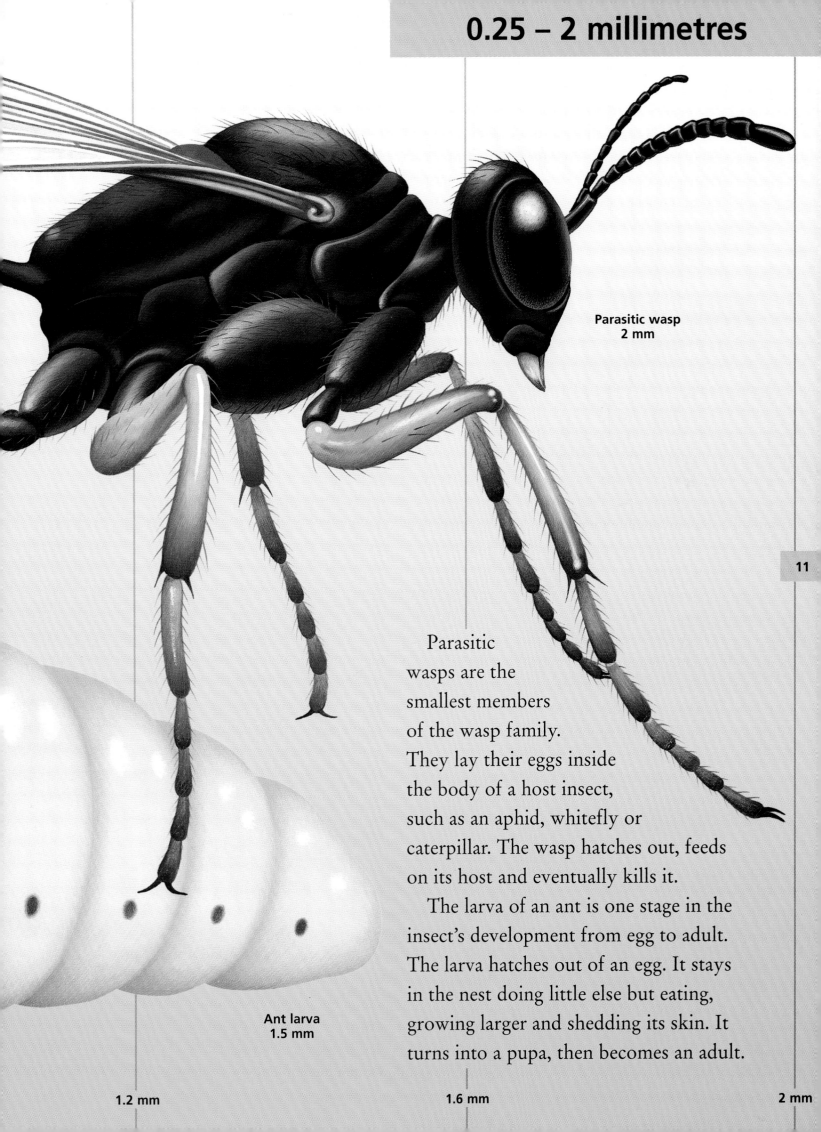

**Parasitic wasp
2 mm**

Parasitic
wasps are the
smallest members
of the wasp family.
They lay their eggs inside
the body of a host insect,
such as an aphid, whitefly or
caterpillar. The wasp hatches out, feeds
on its host and eventually kills it.

The larva of an ant is one stage in the
insect's development from egg to adult.
The larva hatches out of an egg. It stays
in the nest doing little else but eating,
growing larger and shedding its skin. It
turns into a pupa, then becomes an adult.

**Ant larva
1.5 mm**

11

1.2 mm

1.6 mm

2 mm

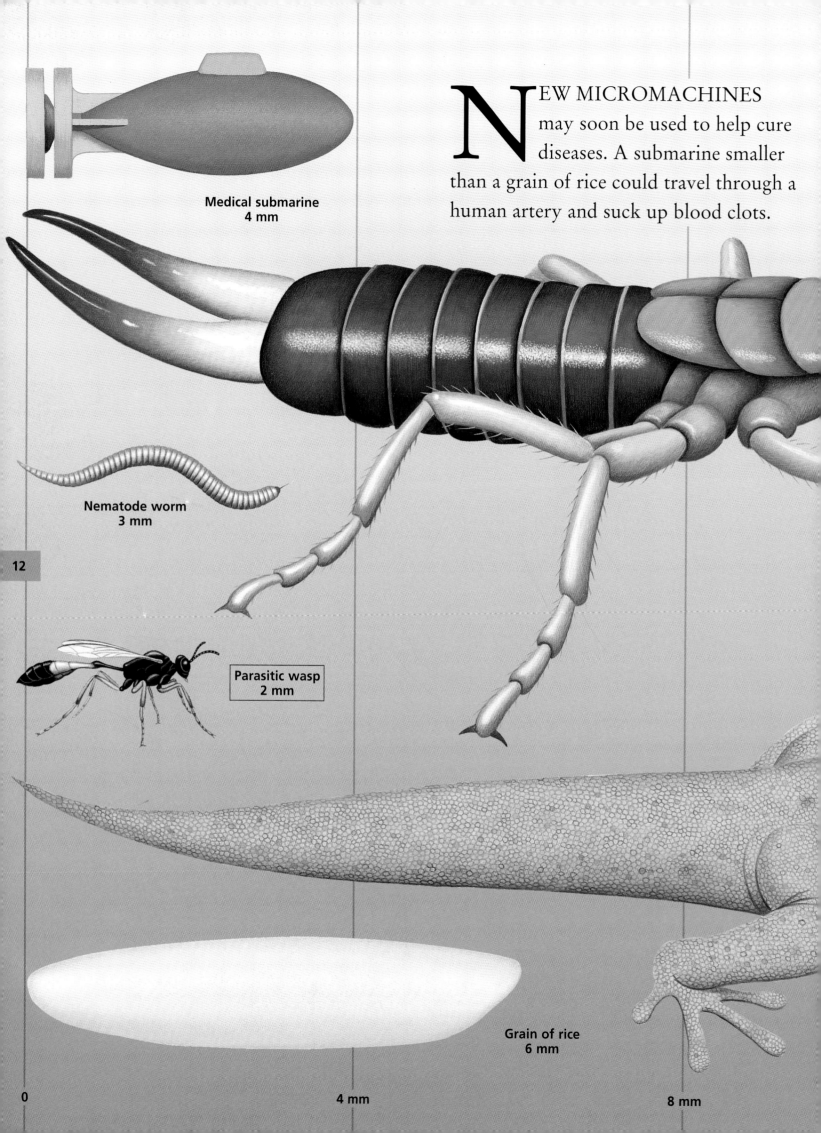

Medical submarine
4 mm

N EW MICROMACHINES
may soon be used to help cure
diseases. A submarine smaller
than a grain of rice could travel through a
human artery and suck up blood clots.

Nematode worm
3 mm

Parasitic wasp
2 mm

Grain of rice
6 mm

0   4 mm   8 mm

Nematode worms can also get inside humans, but their presence is not welcome: they are responsible for many diseases. They are probably the most numerous animals in the world.

Earwigs do *not*, as was once commonly believed, nest in people's ears! But they do prefer to live in narrow crevices. Earwigs eat anything, from other small insects to flowers and plants. They use the strong pincers to capture prey, to protect themselves from their enemies and in mating.

The dwarf gecko is the smallest reptile in the world. Geckos are known for their ability to climb, even on vertical panes of glass. Millions of tiny bristles on their toes help them secure a grip on any surface. Geckos have few defences against predators, apart from their ability to shed their tails if trapped. Most are active only at night—another way of avoiding trouble. Many kinds of nocturnal geckos can make calls. They are often quite loud, repeated chirps and clicks.

**Common earwig
12 mm
(excluding antennae)**

**Dwarf gecko
20 mm**

13

12 mm

20 mm

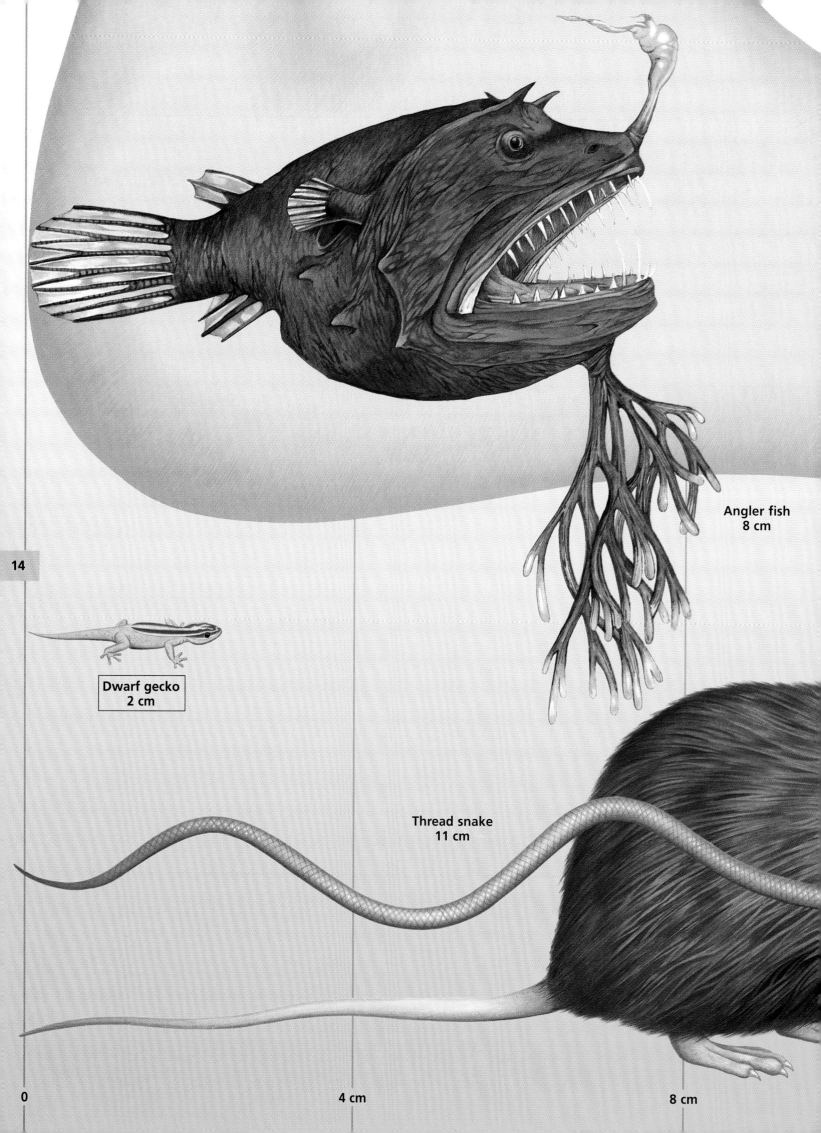

Angler fish
8 cm

14

Dwarf gecko
2 cm

Thread snake
11 cm

0

4 cm

8 cm

LITTLE more than half the length of a child's foot, the thread snake pictured here is completely blind. It spends its life burrowing through the soil in search of ants and termites to eat.

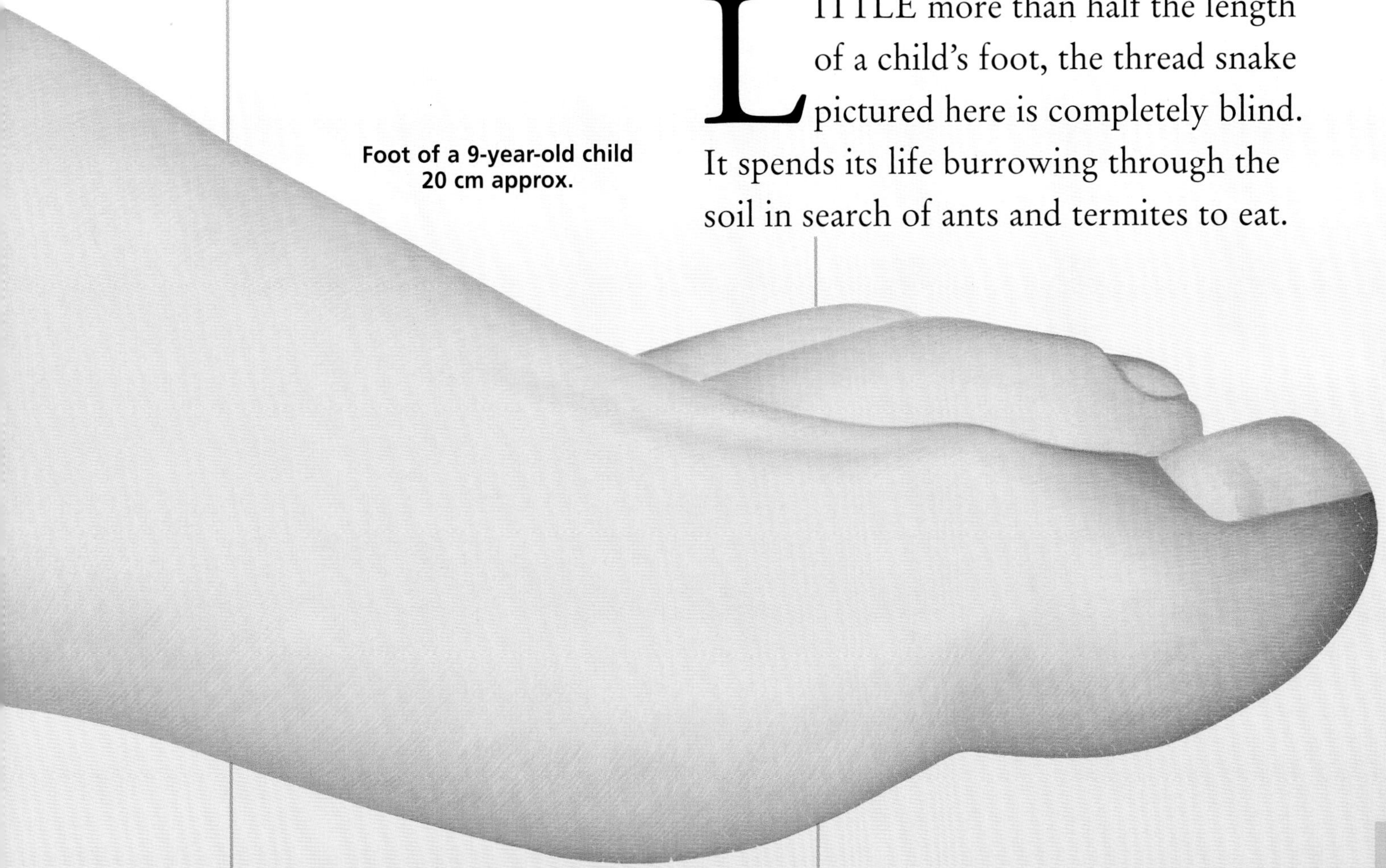

**Foot of a 9-year-old child
20 cm approx.**

The prairie vole is also a burrower. Colonies of these tiny mammals live in large nests, complete with runways and storage chambers, just under the ground in the grasslands of North America.

Some kinds of angler fish may be small, but with their huge mouths lined with long, curved teeth, they are terrifying predators. In the blackness of the deep ocean, an angler fish will use a glowing light, or lure, at the end of its snout, as a bait to attract other small marine creatures, such as fish, squid and crustaceans, towards its gaping jaws ...

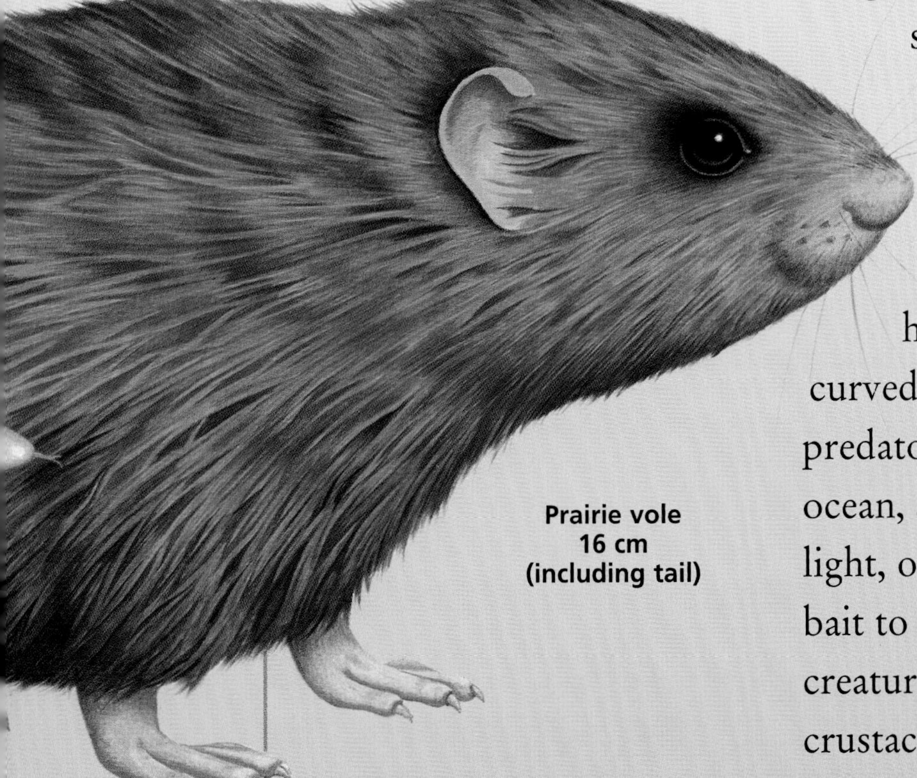

**Prairie vole
16 cm
(including tail)**

12 cm

16 cm

20 cm

Scolopendra
centipede
30 cm

Short-tailed
nurse shark
75 cm

16

Child's foot
20 cm

Duckbilled
platypus
53 cm

0

20 cm

40 cm

NOT ALL dinosaurs were massive. Some of the smallest dinosaurs, such as *Compsognathus*, were about the size of chickens, with only their tails extending

THE LONGEST SHARKS

1	Whale shark	15 metres
2	Basking shark	10 metres
3	Great white shark	7 metres
4	Tiger shark	6 metres
5	Thresher shark	5.5 metres
6	Megamouth	5 metres
7	Prickly shark	4 metres

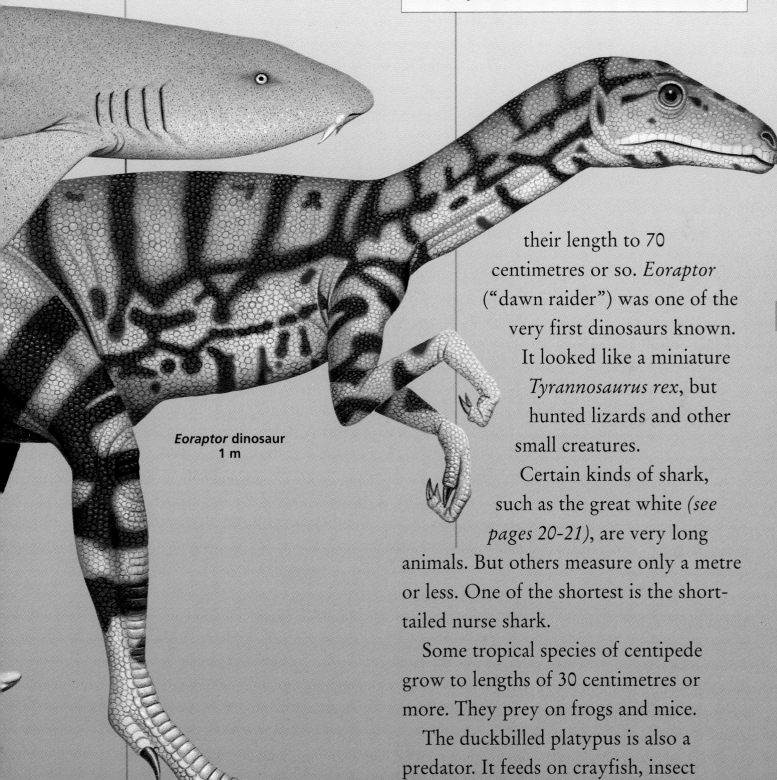

Eoraptor dinosaur
1 m

their length to 70 centimetres or so. *Eoraptor* ("dawn raider") was one of the very first dinosaurs known. It looked like a miniature *Tyrannosaurus rex*, but hunted lizards and other small creatures.

Certain kinds of shark, such as the great white *(see pages 20-21)*, are very long animals. But others measure only a metre or less. One of the shortest is the short-tailed nurse shark.

Some tropical species of centipede grow to lengths of 30 centimetres or more. They prey on frogs and mice.

The duckbilled platypus is also a predator. It feeds on crayfish, insect larvae and snails from the river bed.

17

60 cm

80 cm

1 m

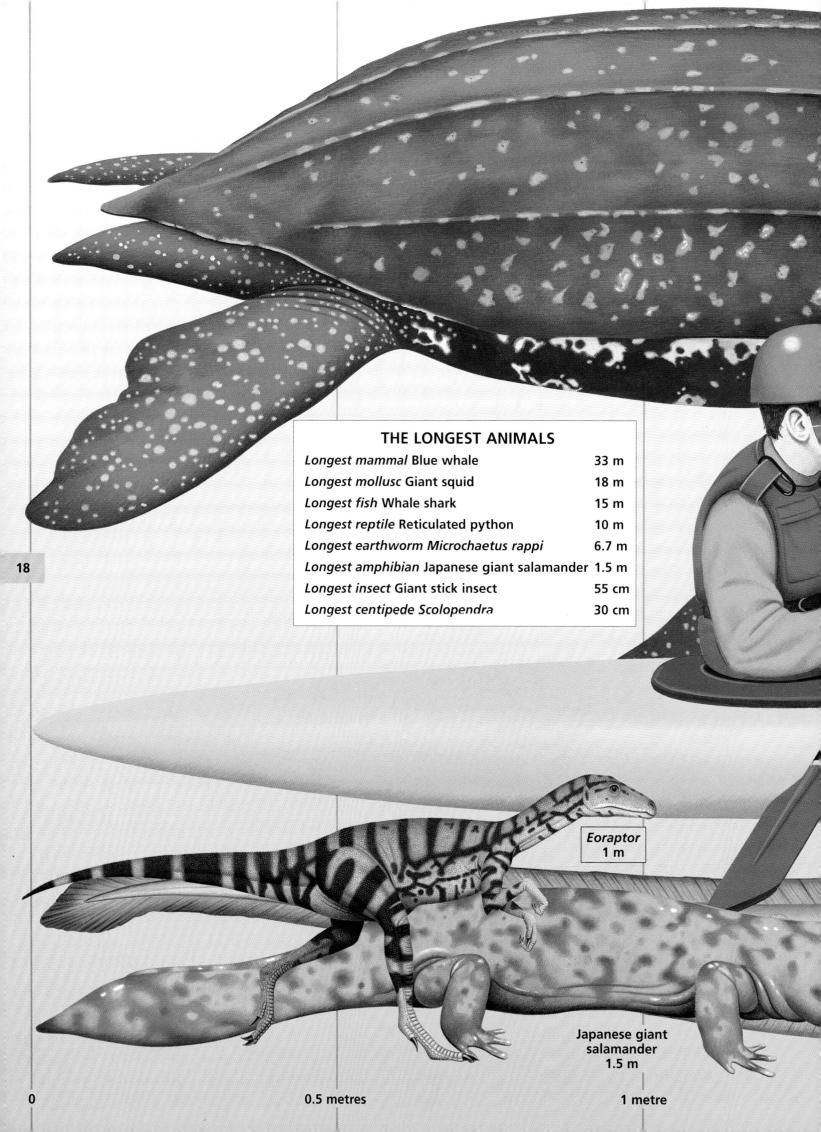

THE LONGEST ANIMALS

Longest mammal Blue whale		33 m
Longest mollusc Giant squid		18 m
Longest fish Whale shark		15 m
Longest reptile Reticulated python		10 m
Longest earthworm Microchaetus rappi		6.7 m
Longest amphibian Japanese giant salamander		1.5 m
Longest insect Giant stick insect		55 cm
Longest centipede Scolopendra		30 cm

Eoraptor
1 m

Japanese giant
salamander
1.5 m

0   0.5 metres   1 metre

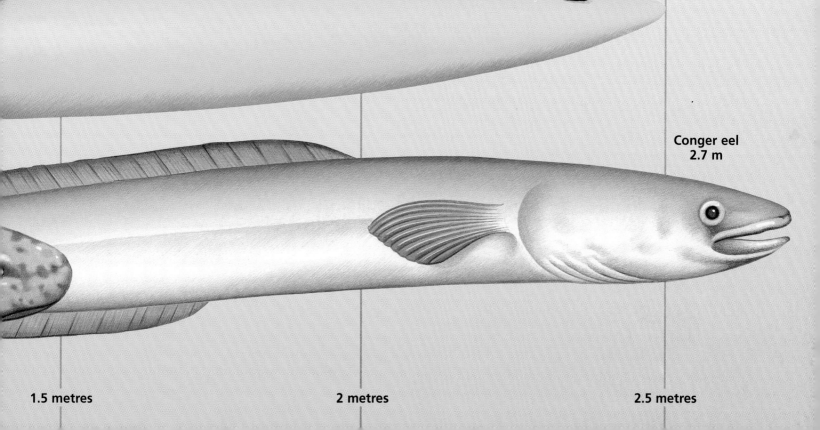

**Leatherback turtle
2 m**

**Single-person canoe
2.5 m**

**Conger eel
2.7 m**

A MPHIBIANS are animals that usually spend most of their lives on land, but breed in the water. The Japanese giant salamander is the largest of all amphibians. It never leaves the water, feeding on other animals in rivers and large streams.

The leatherback turtle is the largest marine turtle. It, too, lives in the water— preying on jellyfish in the deep oceans— but lays its eggs on beaches. On hatching, the young turtles must dash across the sand to the sea. Many are picked off by seabirds and crabs before they get there.

Conger eels have long, slender bodies. They live in shallow waters where they feed on other sea creatures. They lay eggs that hatch into thin, transparent young.

19

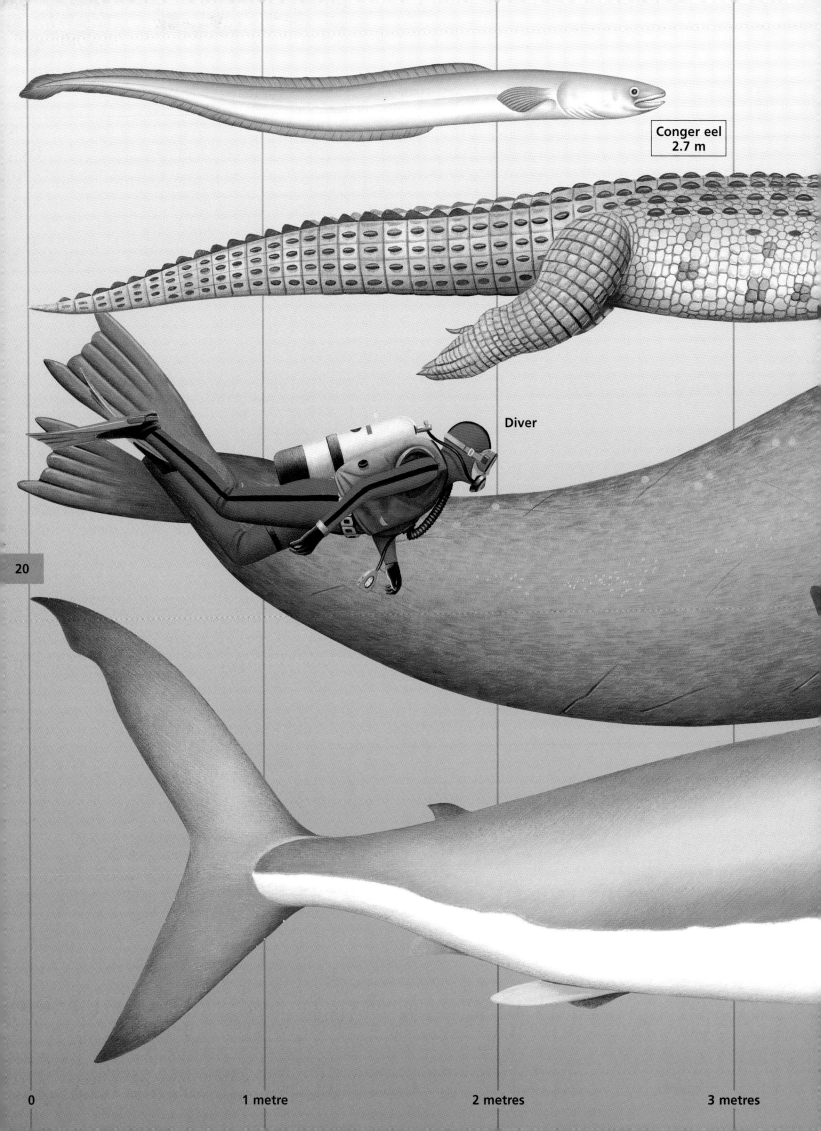

Conger eel
2.7 m

Diver

20

0   1 metre   2 metres   3 metres

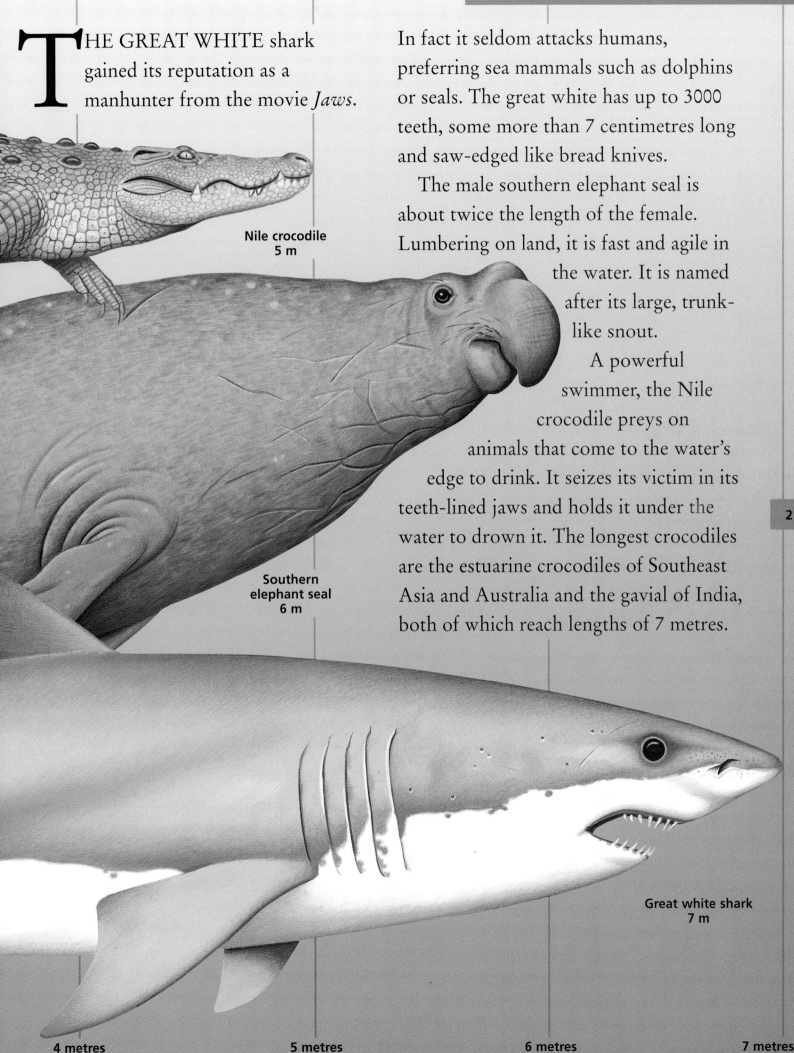

THE GREAT WHITE shark gained its reputation as a manhunter from the movie *Jaws*.

In fact it seldom attacks humans, preferring sea mammals such as dolphins or seals. The great white has up to 3000 teeth, some more than 7 centimetres long and saw-edged like bread knives.

The male southern elephant seal is about twice the length of the female. Lumbering on land, it is fast and agile in the water. It is named after its large, trunk-like snout.

A powerful swimmer, the Nile crocodile preys on animals that come to the water's edge to drink. It seizes its victim in its teeth-lined jaws and holds it under the water to drown it. The longest crocodiles are the estuarine crocodiles of Southeast Asia and Australia and the gavial of India, both of which reach lengths of 7 metres.

Nile crocodile
5 m

Southern
elephant seal
6 m

Great white shark
7 m

21

4 metres   5 metres   6 metres   7 metres

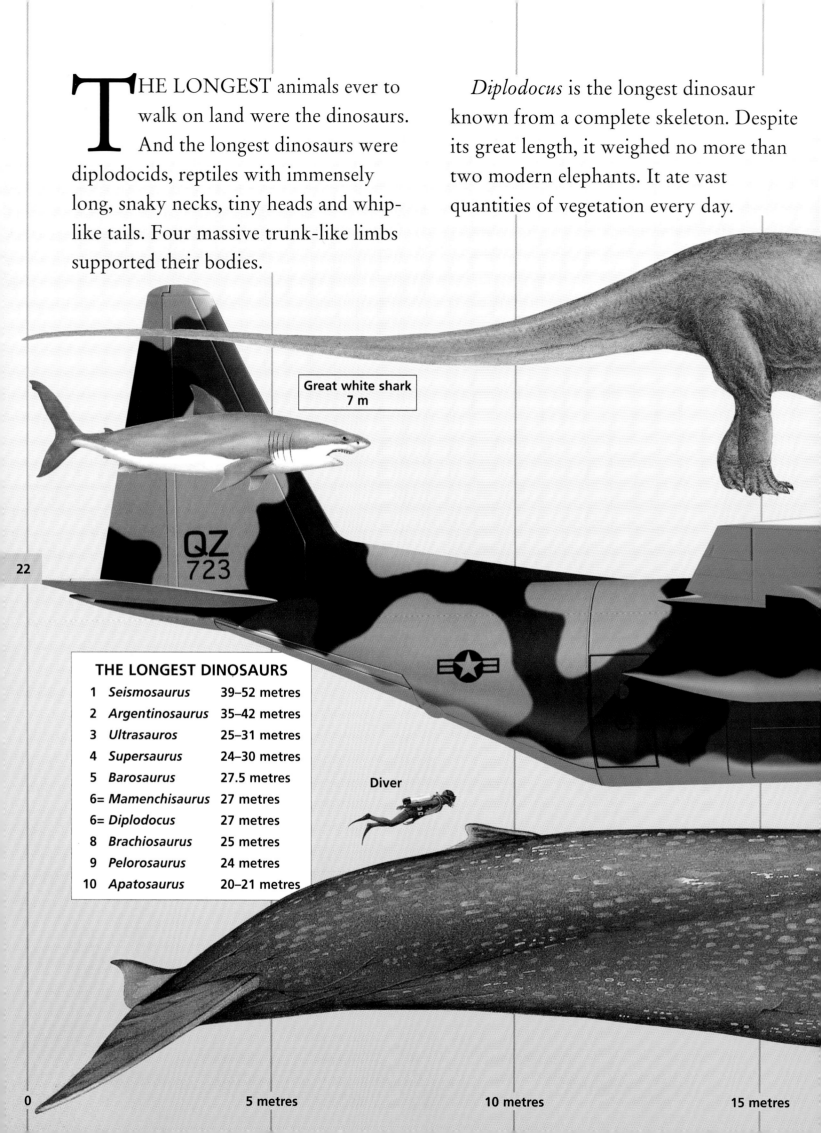

THE LONGEST animals ever to walk on land were the dinosaurs. And the longest dinosaurs were diplodocids, reptiles with immensely long, snaky necks, tiny heads and whip-like tails. Four massive trunk-like limbs supported their bodies.

Diplodocus is the longest dinosaur known from a complete skeleton. Despite its great length, it weighed no more than two modern elephants. It ate vast quantities of vegetation every day.

Great white shark
7 m

QZ
723

THE LONGEST DINOSAURS

1	*Seismosaurus*	39–52 metres
2	*Argentinosaurus*	35–42 metres
3	*Ultrasauros*	25–31 metres
4	*Supersaurus*	24–30 metres
5	*Barosaurus*	27.5 metres
6=	*Mamenchisaurus*	27 metres
6=	*Diplodocus*	27 metres
8	*Brachiosaurus*	25 metres
9	*Pelorosaurus*	24 metres
10	*Apatosaurus*	20–21 metres

Diver

0   5 metres   10 metres   15 metres

Of today's animals, only the blue whale is longer than *Diplodocus*. Other diplodocids, such as *Seismosaurus* for example, may prove to be longer still. Bones discovered so far suggest this dinosaur could have been at least the width of a football pitch!

The blue whale, today a very rare animal, propels itself through the water using its huge tail or fluke. As it goes, it gulps down a daily total of some 40 million krill, tiny, shrimp-like animals that gather in the Southern Ocean. Even a new-born blue whale is a giant—it is about 7 metres long and as heavy as a hippo!

A large male blue whale is actually a little longer than a transport aircraft. The Lockheed C-130 Hercules was specially built to take troops and equipment from place to place. It is big enough to carry army trucks in its hold.

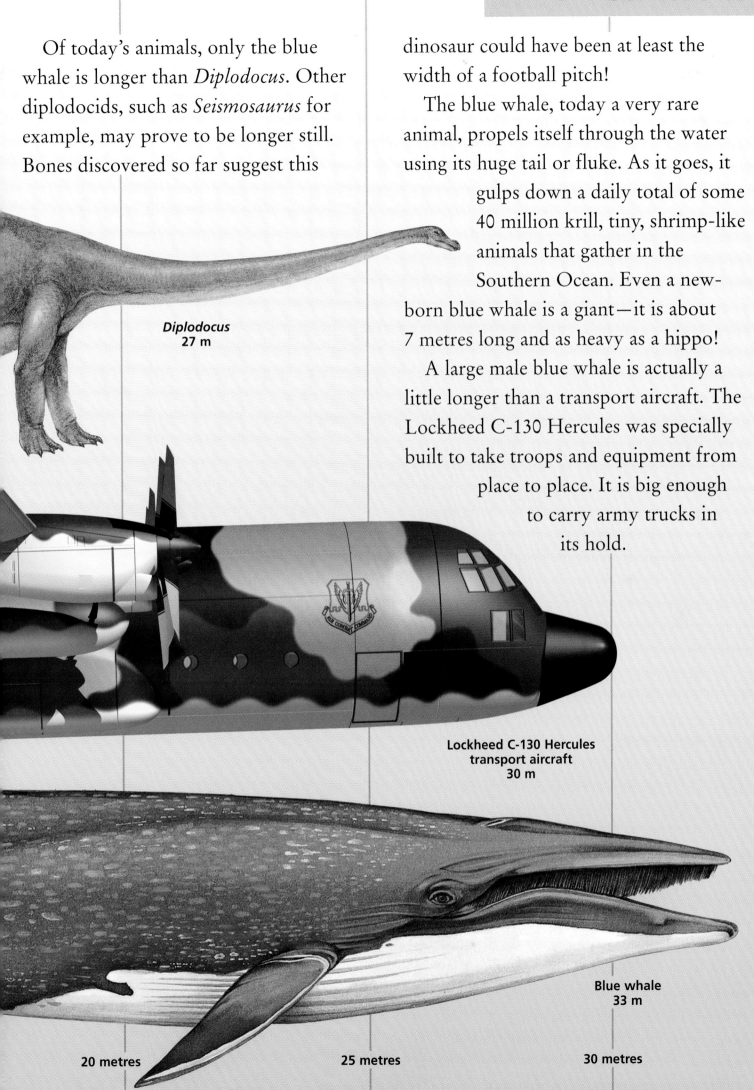

Diplodocus
27 m

Lockheed C-130 Hercules
transport aircraft
30 m

Blue whale
33 m

20 metres

25 metres

30 metres

Clipper City
clipper ship
40 m

**Blue whale
33 m**

0

20 metres

40 metres

**Road train
45 m**

**Boeing 777-200
63.7 m**

American

THE LONGEST WHALES

1	Blue whale	33 m
2	Fin whale	27 m
3	Sei whale	22 m
4	Sperm whale	21 m
5	Northern right whale	17 m
6	Bryde's whale	16 m
7	Grey whale	15.5 m
8	Bowhead whale	15 m
9	Baird's beaked whale	13 m
10	Minke whale	10 m

BLUE WHALES are several times longer than most coaches or lorries—but not as long as road trains. These colossal vehicles, made up of several trailers coupled together, are designed to carry freight or livestock across massive distances in Australia.

The Boeing 777-200 airliner can cover still greater distances: 16,000 kilometres at a time, or about 18 hours in the air. First launched in 1994, this widebody airliner is equipped with the latest technology, called "fly-by wire".

In the late 19th century, the only way to travel around the world was by ship, and the fastest way was in a clipper sailing ship. Designed to travel quickly through the water, clippers were built to carry freight—tea, wool, minerals and timber—as fast as possible across the oceans. Eventually they lost out in competition with large steamships.

The German-built Ambulu ferry was also built for speed. It carries passengers between Indonesian islands at speeds of more than 70 kilometres per hour.

25

**Ambulu passenger
ferry
70 m**

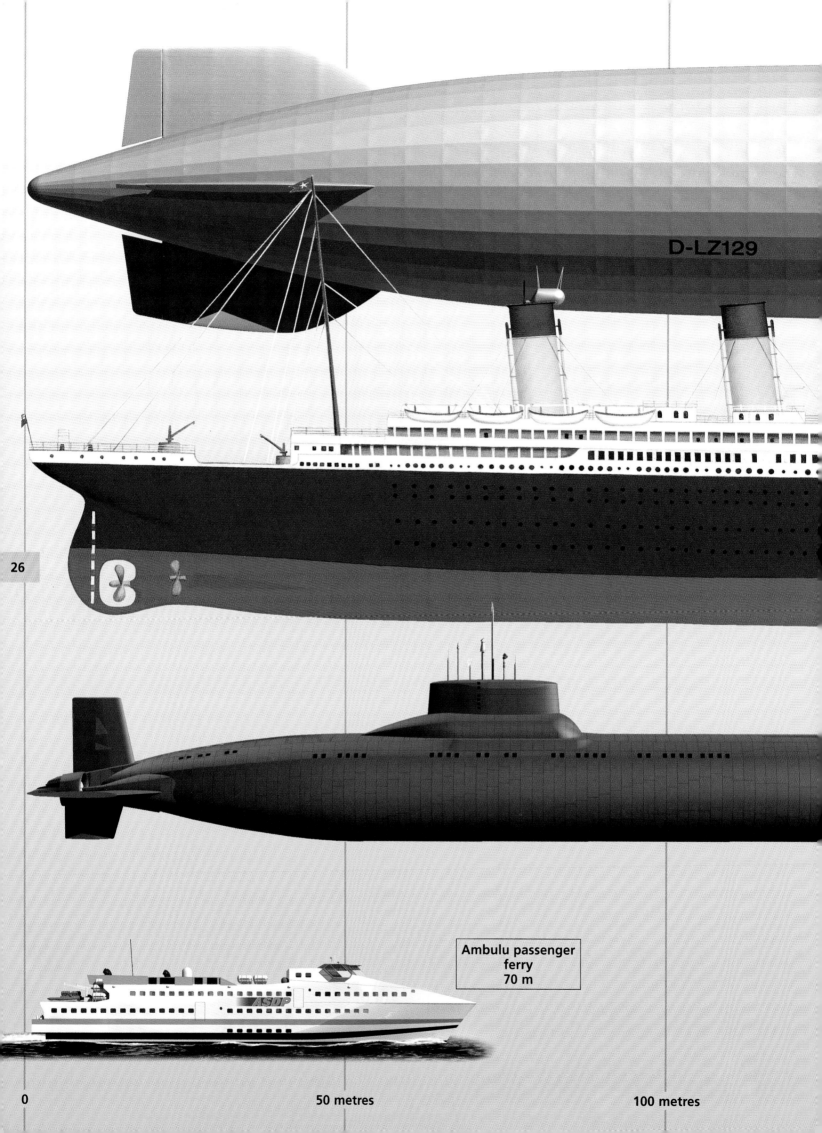

D-LZ129

Ambulu passenger
ferry
70 m

50 metres

100 metres

Hindenburg airship
245 m

Titanic ocean liner
256 m

Soviet Typhoon class
submarine
171 m

27

THE *TITANIC* was the largest ship in the world when she was first launched in 1912. The invention of the steam turbine engine at the end of the 19th century made the building of such large ocean liners possible. The *Titanic* collided with a massive iceberg on her maiden voyage, and sank with the loss of 1502 lives.

The giants of the air at that time were the Zeppelin airships. Larger and larger craft were built, culminating in the massive *Hindenburg* of 1936. It, too, suffered a disastrous end, exploding when landing in New Jersey in 1937, killing 35 people.

The longest submarines ever built were the Soviet Typhoon class vessels. Powered by nuclear reactors, they could stay underwater for years at a time.

150 metres   200 metres   250 metres

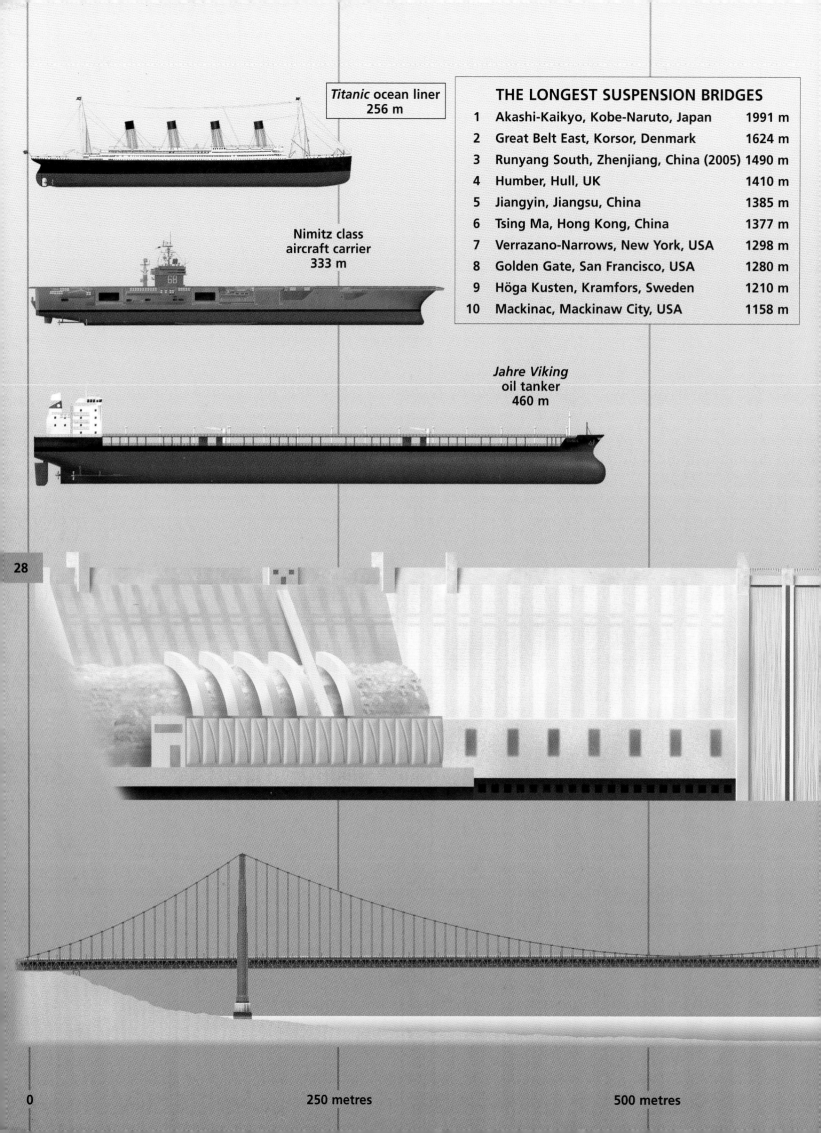

Titanic ocean liner
256 m

Nimitz class
aircraft carrier
333 m

Jahre Viking
oil tanker
460 m

THE LONGEST SUSPENSION BRIDGES

1	Akashi-Kaikyo, Kobe-Naruto, Japan	1991 m
2	Great Belt East, Korsor, Denmark	1624 m
3	Runyang South, Zhenjiang, China (2005)	1490 m
4	Humber, Hull, UK	1410 m
5	Jiangyin, Jiangsu, China	1385 m
6	Tsing Ma, Hong Kong, China	1377 m
7	Verrazano-Narrows, New York, USA	1298 m
8	Golden Gate, San Francisco, USA	1280 m
9	Höga Kusten, Kramfors, Sweden	1210 m
10	Mackinac, Mackinaw City, USA	1158 m

28

0   250 metres   500 metres

OCEAN LINERS and aircraft carriers are very long ships, but the longest of all are oil tankers. Four football pitches could be laid out end to end on the deck of the *Jahre Viking*, the record-holder, and there would still be room to spare. A ship of this size cannot be brought to a stop inside a distance of less than 6 kilometres.

The Nimitz class aircraft carriers of the US Navy are the largest warships of all. Each can carry more than 90 aircraft and travel more than 2 million kilometres without refuelling.

Work started on the Grand Coulee Dam in Washington State, USA, in 1933. As tall as a 46-storey building, it was built to dam the Columbia River and provide water to a large area of desert land—known as the coulee country. Some of the water in the reservoir is allowed to rush out through pipes and make turbines spin, producing electricity.

The Golden Gate Bridge, San Francisco, USA, was first opened to traffic in 1938. At the time, it had the world's longest span. The overall length, including approaches, is 2738 metres.

**Grand Coulee Dam
1272 m**

**Golden Gate Bridge
1280 m span**

750 metres   **1000 metres**   **1250 metres**

A

aircraft, transport 23
aircraft carriers, Nimitz class 28-29
airliners 25
airships 27
Ambulu passenger ferry 25, 26
amphibian, world's longest 18-19
angler fish 14-15
animals,
    world's longest 18
    world's most numerous 13
ant larva 11

B

bacteria 6-7, 8-9
beetle, feather-winged 9, 10
beetles, world's smallest 9
Boeing 777-200 25

C

canoe 19
centipedes 17
child, foot of 15, 16
clipper ship 24-25
Compsognathus 17
crocodile, Nile 21

D

dinosaurs 17, 22-23
    world's longest 22

Diplodocus 22-23
diver 20, 22

EF

E. coli 7
earwig, common 13
eel, conger 19, 20
Eoraptor 17, 18
ferries 25

GHJ

gecko, dwarf 13, 14
Golden Gate Bridge 28-29
Grand Coulee Dam 29
Hindenburg 27
Jahre Viking 28-29

LM

living things, world's smallest 7
Lockheed C-130 Hercules 23
micromachines 12
microscopic objects 7, 9
mite, dust 10

OPR

ocean liners 27, 29
oil tankers 29
platypus, duckbilled 16-17
rice, grain of 12
road train 25

S

salamander, Japanese giant 18-19
Scolopendra 16
seal, southern elephant 21
Seismosaurus 22-23
shark,
    great white 17, 21, 22
    short-tailed nurse 16-17
    whale 17, 18
sharks, world's longest 17
snake, thread 14-15
submarine,
    medical 12
    Typhoon class 27
    world's longest 27
suspension bridges, world's
    longest 28

TV

tardigrade (water bear) 9
Titanic 27, 28
turtle, leatherback 19
virus 6-7
vole, prairie 15

W

wasp, parasitic 11, 12
water bear *see* tardigrade
whale, blue 18, 23, 24-25
whales, world's longest 25
worm, nematode 12-13